Investment secrets

long-term

Content

- Cautions when investing in cryptocurrencies 5
- What to keep in mind when investing in cryptocurrencies for the long term ... 10
- Is it profitable to invest in cryptocurrencies in the long term? 14
- Speculation when investing long-term in cryptocurrencies 17
- The Bitcoin price with a long term view 19
- How you can build your cryptocurrency portfolio for the long term 21
- Can cryptocurrencies be long-term investments? 31
- Forming a long-term cryptocurrency investment strategy 33
- Examples and visions for long-term investment in cryptocurrencies 52
- Most effective strategies when investing in Cardano 57
- What to keep in mind when investing in cryptocurrencies for the long term ... 60
- Considerations and doubts about long-term trading 68
- The investment role of social trading 72
- The "HODL or die" trend 77
- Measures to invest in Bitcoin for the long term 78

Long-term investments in cryptocurrencies are in trend due to the large number of users who bet on this way, although it is a volatile option, it is also true that there are testimonies of success that attract anyone, but you should know the best strategies to make the best decisions.

You must keep an open mind to learn more and more about this environment, because cryptocurrencies are generating an important boom, with exorbitant results, as well as considerable losses, so you can not take anything for granted, or stop taking risks to obtain a positive margin for your life.

Cautions when investing in cryptocurrencies

When thinking about cryptocurrencies as a long-term investment measure, don't forget to consider certain forecasts, as on the one hand there is the broad appeal of a digital currency like Bitcoin reaching over $40,000 USD, but many may describe it as a trajectory of ups and downs where you must be patient.

Through some market movement, an unpredictable change can be generated on the value of some cryptocurrency, surpassing your expectations completely, or, on the other hand, it can destroy any illusion, they are quotes that can go for or against you, in the case of Bitcoin it had its skeptical lapses until an explosion.

But the example of this pioneer cryptocurrency, lets you know how active this medium is, where market trends are the ones that impose conditions, from 2018 onwards investments on these assets have skyrocketed, and with those same investments the price of cryptocurrencies has changed.

The current cryptocurrency market is going through a much more mature and conscious stage, where the participation of institutional media also stands out, which is why it is a reliable scenario for different users, although it is still a space where at any moment an asset can collapse or go up.

The volatile spark of cryptocurrencies does not disappear, but there are certain steps that can help you regulate what happens, since with a series of alternatives you can have more confidence in case of any event, so you should know the following provisions when making your investment:

1. **Acquire sufficient experience**

It may seem a basic recommendation, but within each financial market knowledge and experience is required to make decisions, in addition to assuming to live with the risk that volatility implies, especially when it comes to crypto, where more precautions should be taken into account.

There is no doubt that over time Bitcoin has been responsible for demonstrating the variability of a price, but this should not scare anyone away, because every market has risks, although the advantage lies on the look into the future, as it is a profitable alternative in the long term, for the various positive results exposed.

The volatility that exists within this area can favor you in the long term, because the appreciation is more likely to undergo a rise than a fall, but the important thing to accept is that the risk is not only on the currency, but on the starting force that they have, so they can collapse any market and repeatedly.

For this reason, evaluation is a faculty that every investor must have, since it allows you to determine if the asset meets the appropriate profile for investment, as well as you yourself must submit yourself to questioning to measure your pulse, especially understanding that you will be part of a highly volatile market.

Mastering this unpredictable aspect can be complicated for some investors, this is due to the inexperience in this sector, they completely increase the importance of the previous analysis of what you are going to find or what you will be subjected to, therefore it is not a recommended alternative for beginners, you must have a previous base.

2. **Don't put all your funds in a single asset.**

The starting point for investing, and especially for deciding the type of asset on which you are going to bet, is by thoroughly researching what it means to invest in digital assets, as this allows you to master and work with all the risks that arise from the level of volatility that abounds in the market.

In addition to the volatile level of the market, you must take into account and know that there are more than 7,000 digital currencies, but not all of them work or fit with a long-term investment, likewise not all of them manage to survive, so when entering this market, you must inform yourself about the function of the cryptocurrency that catches your attention.

By thoroughly understanding everything behind this asset, you can invest with greater clarity, you can put into practice any guidelines or rules over traditional investments, for this reason it is fundamental that you can invest in a diversified way, instead of just dedicating all your funds on the same cryptocurrency.

In the case of the most professional investors, they recommend or use a pattern of allocating a part of their portfolio, i.e. only use 5% or 10% of a market, the distribution of the percentage has many modalities or practices, the usual is to dedicate 80% to the one that generates confidence and 15% to the rest of an asset or assets.

3. **Follow closely the news and technical analysis**

When you are part of the cryptocurrency market, you can't stop consulting everything that happens nowadays, because an asset has movements around the news, this can be as susceptible as a rumor, or a simple tweet, as it happens constantly with Elon Musk, which directly influences Bitcoin or Dogecoin.

It is an environment where anything goes, for that reason you must keep the filters active to recognize what is happening within the industry, reading each information with that perspective can take action on your investment, especially if it is about upcoming releases.

Beyond celebrities, there are more factors that move the market, as certain hedge funds exert some influence and are part of those news that cause a stir on the market, because volatility depends on these types of factors or variables, but it does not mean that you should abandon technical analysis.

In a day there are a large number of movements, which leave a trail known as volume that can be studied to detect any incidence, because behind the price change of an asset can be evidenced a number of positions to exploit at the time of investing.

What to keep in mind when investing in cryptocurrencies for the long term

Investing in cryptocurrencies in the long term can become a profitable decision, although it is a huge market that you must know in depth, as long as you take into account some data you can follow that kind of guidance, although this form of virtual investment allows you to investigate each form of operation.

The important thing is that it is not a centralized form, but on the contrary, banks or institutions do not intervene, but it is about algorithms, which allow the purchase and sale to be simple, where an attractive level of security and speed is manifested in comparison with other assets.

High value is a huge wake-up call, so you should know the following points as one of the first steps to start investing:

- **Measures to invest in cryptocurrencies**

A general rule is to start investing little so you can learn from your mistakes, it also helps to reduce any level of anxiety that you may be presenting, it is essential that you do not get ahead of yourself and have patience when you start, this is the best way to find and develop strategies associated with trade.

On the other hand, as it has been reiterated, preparation is everything before making an important step, so you should research about blockchain technology, which is developed by means of a unique registry, and is what allows the movement of digital currencies, as it is also vital to know about circulating supply vs. total currencies.

The circulation of currencies is composed of those that are generated as well as those that are available in existence, this is known as inflation, which involves the exchange of wallets, both public and private keys, mastering this allows you to limit any problems in the future when investing.

So the trick is to read as much as you can, that way you can take more concrete steps when investing in cryptocurrencies, this is part of the essence of the market, and in the future is a measure that will help you not to lose money, as you learn you will be much more confident in your decisions.

Experience can be gained by reading, and understanding each of your mistakes, it is also a risky path, but little by little you can do excellent, once you find a good investment that is part of these digital currencies, where at each step you need to evaluate the type of exchange to be made.

You can take as much time as it takes, there is no rush because everything depends on your convenience, appealing for attractive rates because no matter how big or small the investment is you should aim for positive results, but you should never invest more than you are willing to lose.

- **The cryptocurrencies with the greatest attention or popularity on the market**

The trading activity of each cryptocurrency is highly profitable, although you need to follow closely some impositions for you to understand everything behind a sale or purchase, as this has direct impact on cryptocurrencies, trading in general lines has some fixed opportunities or alternatives.

One of the best incidences about cryptocurrencies is that of Ethereum, since it has become one of the largest cryptocurrencies in terms of capitalization, it was created in 2014, this also serves as a platform and uses the Ether coin, a currency that is kept working with Smart Contracts.

On the other hand, the importance of Bitcoin is still valid as it is one of the first, so it has a valuable footprint in the market, since 2009 it has grown completely under a supply cap of 21 million bitcoins, when transacting with them an anonymous operation is developed, so customers do not identify such transactions.

Thirdly, the startup is parked on Litecoin, as it is part of the Bitcoin project, it works as a fully decentralized global network with payments developed through open source, this cryptocurrency is used much more in instant transactions, or can be used to buy other cryptocurrencies.

Investing in cryptocurrencies is a wide world of opportunities, digital money is part of the future, so sticking to a thorough knowledge of the market can leave you with better dividends, profits are just a step away from you.

Is it profitable to invest in cryptocurrencies in the long term?

Investing in any cryptocurrency, especially the likes of Bitcoin is considered one of the most volatile, due to the fact that prices are subject to different fluctuations, but this does not mean that it ceases to be a highly attractive asset, especially when compared to physical assets.

Different analysts hold a full belief about investing in cryptocurrencies in the long term, this is known as Hodl, which means that you should hold the cryptocurrency instead of selling it, understanding the principle that cryptocurrencies are much more convenient investments for individuals than for companies.

Cryptocurrencies are usually doubted because of the kind of controversies surrounding them, but also other aspects drive the level of volatility, including on asset prices, which can be interpreted as an unstable ecosystem, to the point that they are not well regarded in the eyes of some investors.

Beyond the controversies surrounding cryptocurrencies, you can progressively approach long-term investments, being a great alternative with a high but acceptable degree of risk, the only drawback to keep in mind is that in the long term you can face market price drops.

Sharp falls are the only enemies, as they possess direct incidence on cryptocurrency prices, because it is a broad crypto market and assets change as part of Blockchain technology for being a weapon of the future, in the midst of this offering is the possibility of:

- **Cryptocurrency trading**

The investment of cryptocurrencies, becomes a reality under the function of cryptocurrency trading, where you can sell and buy to take advantage of the fluctuations that are developing, this can be done from any wallet as they are specialized agents for this purpose.

Among the most popular trading options are Binance, Coinbase Pro, Poloniex, Kraken, Bitfine and Bitrex.

- **Long-term investment in crypto assets**

What they represent to long-term investments, they are classified as blockchain projects as a long-term view, but which is developed as an ERC 20 type in the middle of the Ethereum blockchain, is a type of investment that demands a high level of knowledge, comparatively as is investment in venture capital funds.

• Pension fund for cryptocurrencies

Some institutions are beginning to bet on creating a fund based on crypto assets, intended for pensions to have a digital currency asset manager, this becomes a breakthrough for institutions, as it allows to create a retirement account, to the point of being investors in cryptocurrencies.

Investing in a cryptocurrency fund can generate important results in the future, more and more people are motivated to take this step, which can result in a successful investment that gives you peace of mind, this kind of influence is being presented on the cryptocurrency market.

There is no doubt that investing in cryptocurrencies in the long term, as long as you can assume the risk, the rest is to maintain a persistent and patient term, especially for some positive return to arise in your favor.

Speculation when investing long-term in cryptocurrencies

Every major investor includes cryptocurrencies as an important livelihood nowadays, especially because it is an asset that revaluates in the long term, leaving good dividends on portfolios, therefore cryptocurrencies are seen as a store of value, just as gold was in its time.

Between Bitcoin and Ethereum, they are known as the biggest assets in the world, due to their exorbitant level of ascent, where every month they surpassed their prices or values, challenging any forecast, but it is also true that they decline drastically, like Bitcoin, hovering above $40,000 USD and then dropping to $35,000 USD.

These demonstrations are a clear example of the level of volatility, throughout its history these scenarios have been repeated, but at the same time it is one of the reasons why it is attractive, since speculation can be used to your advantage, this component is a temptation to generate a percentage of profit.

The paradigms around cryptocurrencies have changed and they prefer this way over traditional institutions, where skeptics leave open the possibility of trading in this way, which is a protection from inflation that you can urge on some kind of centralized financial institution.

This asset is able to overcome all types of speculation, therefore it is integrated as a type of long-term investment portfolio, beyond any change in the market, these assets manage to stay healthy in terms of profit, they are investments that translate into multi-asset, although the enemy to overcome is that barrier of withdrawing too soon.

Most certainly the long term view needs support, with a positive outlook on the asset, that is what allows that in the future some new upside can be successfully harvested, that is what consolidates the level of profit you generate, this is a direction studied on a large scale to follow bullish trends.

On the other hand, a price drop can be taken advantage of to increase the kind of profit you make, since it is used as an economic price to harvest eye-catching percentages, so it is a favorable option even for retailers, it is an explicit potential on the store of value, it is a kind of virtual gold.

The ability of a cryptocurrency to set aside inflation is very important, it is a kind of modern safe haven, therefore these financial assets allow a wide diversification of investments, it is a way to make the most of the speculative side, in the midst of the upside you can track Bitcoin and Ethereum.

Everything that drags a cryptocurrency is notorious about its movements, but it is a march that works up or down, at some point the rises have reached record highs, in this aspect is that the similarities and differences of each cryptoasset are distinguished, the role of each is housed behind the value of the same.

The Bitcoin price with a long term view

The cryptocurrency market, being unregulated, acquires a high level of visibility, but is in direct contact with a significant amount of fluctuations, so in the case of wanting to closely follow the growth of Bitcoin, or any other, it is common to deal with a margin of risk.

There is very little regulation on cryptocurrencies, this for many may be a huge attraction, while for others it may represent total insecurity, but at least it is a means of payment that acquires more power, besides being classified as a bidirectional medium because it can be exchanged for a traditional currency such as dollar or euro.

Short-term market variability is influenced by any type of media factor, but when aspirations persist to pursue a long-term investment, you can follow this comparison that illustrates any fears you may have:

- **The influence of regulation on the price of Bitcoin**

Some falls that Bitcoin has suffered are related or have coincided with some regulatory measures, which has caused some rumors to arise that when control measures are introduced, there will be a fall in its price, due to the fact that transactions will be much more measured.

Added to this is the ban on trading cryptocurrencies that has been implemented in some countries, which also caused a lower price on Bitcoin, due to the fear of losing the money invested because of the measure dictated, but some other news such as the more positive exchange position of the European Union have caused an upswing.

So far this is the most decisive point or factor on the price or quotation of Bitcoin, the rest is news of large companies or services that are linking or unlinking to this means of payment, but in general terms it has been one of the most reliable cryptocurrencies.

How you can build your cryptocurrency portfolio for the long term

An investment strategy in cryptocurrencies is an excellent planning, in this medium highlights the long-term option which can become a reality after more than 7,000 cryptoassets in the market, you can choose freely and go experimenting little by little with the necessary fundamentals that this market demands.

The choice of a cryptocurrency can really make you a millionaire, but the steps to follow are related to the expansion of the portfolio, in addition to knowing how to use some instruments in the long term, all this is answered through market research, this step is constant and a novice can become an expert.

A long term cryptocurrency portfolio can be formed, after some basic concepts that will allow you to stay on top, in addition to forming and studying a list of cryptocurrencies that facilitate investment, the first concept to discover is the advantages and then the cons.

1. Concepts to be followed in the long term

The investments that are carried out in the long term, awaiting the intention of selling this asset in the future, it can be about a year or any other measure you wish, this is known under the term of hodling, in fact, it is used as a synonym for a long-term investment.

But this term, possesses the belief that betting on an asset that is capable of reaching the moon, becomes a viable strategy, especially because some reliable measures or data, are responsible for confirming this fact, it is the same thing that happens with conventional investments.

The cryptocurrency industry sustains a volatile nature, because changes arise on a constant basis but at the same time implies a high risk, since assets are subject to a drastic mobility, which at the same time provides profits from so many changes.

A purchase made today may lose its validity in the course of the year, this is thanks to the volatility factor, that is why a deep study of cryptographic events is required, that kind of dynamics is what provides profits, but in the long term it is an investment path with a lower risk margin.

When you want to take a first step in cryptocurrencies, in the long run it is a positive methodology for newbies, but you must have constant participation so that there is a greater compatibility with the cryptocurrency portfolio, since the requirement is to master these environments.

2. **Benefits of long-term investments in cryptocurrencies**

The level of crypto volatility allows to raise the value of crypto investments consecutively, this at the same time means that you can build a project itself in the future, following the cause that there is about the asset or what it represents for the world, thus you will be a more active participant in the market.

On the other hand, when it comes to long-term investments, it is advisable to pay attention to those that are emerging, because this type of holding is a sign of considerable gains in the future, as happened with Bitcoin and the investors who believed in it from the beginning.

One advantage of its qualities as an asset is that it has no imposition of central authority, meaning that central control is placed on the users so that they are able to take advantage of its decentralized composition, so that no government is able to deflate the value or inflate it.

3. The disadvantages of investing in cryptocurrencies in the long term

The downside of long-term cryptocurrency investments is that some inflation or volatility can devalue the future, in the case of cryptocurrency qualities are based on digital assets, which are exposed to some kind of hacking on the wallets, as well as tracking the portfolio.

The access to a wallet that holds the funds can be lost or vulnerable, due to forgetting a password, or some kind of hacking, so you must choose an environment that is totally reliable.

4. Builds a cryptocurrency portfolio

The decision to invest in cryptocurrencies must have a clear vision that you are going to keep, that is, if you want to keep it for a long time you need to investigate some basic points, it is a step by step that facilitates a better outcome, first of all, you must choose a cryptocurrency on which you are going to invest.

The choice of the cryptocurrency requires a thorough research on the asset, so that you can establish your own personal criteria, to study the evolution of the asset in the long term, it is required to devote full attention to the reputation behind the currency.

The best consultation you can do is through social networks, but above all to take into account the opinion of some users who have experience in the world of cryptocurrencies, this allows you to get to the second step as it is the research of the main idea on which the asset is based.

As long as a cryptocurrency can be focused on solving Blockchain technology problems, it means that there is a future backed by a vision that allows the asset to grow, meaning that the asset has a solid foundation to become the highest point in an industry.

You should ask yourself, if such cryptocurrency gets all your attention, this is simple to determine by means of the market capitalization of the cryptocurrency, this means that the market share of a digital asset is checked, the higher the capitalization, the less risk it implies for an investor.

The experience of investing in this type of market is acquired through portfolio diversification, following the general rule of not placing all your capital on a single asset, especially when it comes to long-term investments, so buying at least two cryptoassets in the long term can keep you more confident.

The data that exists is understood as the chances of an asset to increase in value, since those are the profits you want to pursue, once that step is passed the next thing is to determine the cryptocurrency portfolio tracker, for this you can implement some tools that provide detailed information.

That kind of service that works like a browser, can be found through Cryptocompare or Cointracker is also useful, as they are comprehensive utilities that allow you to track your investments, in the long run they also allow you to have a digital wallet that is multi-currency in nature, it must be safe and secure.

5. **The type of cryptocurrency you can choose from**

When building a cryptocurrency portfolio, one step mentioned above is the analysis of the market, as this makes it easier to measure the type of options that exist for investment, looking for some alternative that is promising, thus the potential can be measured even in a type of categories that help to measure preferences.

Creating the portfolio starts from these main cryptocurrencies, which function as essential pillars due to the level of capitalization they represent and the influence they are capable of exerting. In the case of Bitcoin, it is an alternative that moves the entire world with every movement, and is a reasonable investment choice.

On the other hand, a powerful cryptocurrency type such as Ethereum (ETH), which drives decentralized exchanges, as a highly valuable evolution within the market because it is a variable on the blockchain, which in turn sustains the value of ETH and becomes a highly valuable instrument to kickstart the portfolio.

But in this market you can come across some anonymous cryptocurrencies, as it is a type of asset where identity is taken care of which at the same time provides privacy for all kinds of users about the transactions, this modality has demand on this market, because the world is sticking to more technological blockchains.

The adoption and bets for this kind of cryptocurrencies reach an increasing number, for this reason the study of this aspect causes that anonymous digital assets are more appreciated and invested as part of the daily routine, one of the most popular cryptocurrencies that guarantee privacy is Zcash, which allows all kinds of operations.

A point to study in depth is the protocol of cryptocurrencies, since in the midst of assets promising projects are developed on a global scale, this started by means of Initial Coin Offerings (ICO), this is currently deactivated, since it is announced as a scam, but there are projects that have technological solutions.

One of the current decentralized trends is set up over a demanded industry, it possesses the main motivation of joining real-world applications along with smart contracts, in this regard Chainlink has been growing strikingly over the cryptocurrency lists.

In the case of Polkadot, it is developed under a market that has a high level of credibility, thanks to the fact that it is a platform that has all kinds of solutions when making interchain transfers, even attacking scalability problems, because the DOT currency is also a good option in the long term.

In this same sense, Cardano (ADA) stands out, since it is the result of a broad project to reinforce some central problems behind blockchain technology, such as the lack of scalability, increasing the level of transaction speed, as a sign of security and transparency.

The reputation of this type of cryptocurrency is impeccable, therefore, since it has a high market capitalization, it has a high potential to issue solutions to any event, this ADA coin fits completely with the strategies of the cryptocurrency portfolio.

An asset to follow closely is MIOTA, as it is known as an asset of great relevance, although there is a detail behind the IOTA cryptocurrency is the way it operates, because it has no commission or miners, because the developers of the project formed a self-sufficient network that is scalable and allows confirming transactions.

This kind of project does not work through Blockchain technology, but uses a form of consensus such as Tangle, but retains the other qualities of digital currencies, such as decentralization, encryption methods and no external control.

An interesting option to measure is NEO, which has ample advantages that have generated confidence, to the point of positioning itself as one of the main currencies in terms of the number of total market capitalization, other alternatives that you can investigate is Tron and EOS, since its creation has a native blockchain.

But the market situation is still a major factor, so having a portfolio of promising measures that can reduce some kind of loss is a job that helps you to increase payments and even decrease the fees that exist on international transactions.

The use of XLM leaves an open door on companies, since it is used by companies that have millionaire capitalizations, at the same time it does not cease to be an economic cryptocurrency, its movements signal a frequent upward trend as its typical development.

A fast version of all that Bitcoin represents is Litecoin, where it is part of the first or main cryptocurrencies of the moment, and its movements suggest that it is a sustainable behavior, so it can be an ideal long-term purchase, especially to implement some predictive signal which is useful.

A cryptocurrency with a long journey is Bitcoin Cash, as it is one of the forks that allow it to be a cryptocurrency with the largest market capitalization, but it is an industry that provides a large number of assets for you to choose the one you find most reliable for your plans.

Each cryptocurrency has a different and special offer, and its purchase is simpler with the type of technology that is currently involved in each financial step, you can invest as long as you keep in mind the degree of volatility to which you will be exposed.

Can cryptocurrencies be long-term investments?

Entering the field of cryptocurrencies can raise a lot of questions, the main one being whether they are a good financial instrument to bet on in the long term, which has been explained by experts who are clearly confident in the growth potential that each cryptocurrency has shown.

The consideration of these virtual currencies is due to its wide investment option, but in the long term it may be an important question to leave aside, within this topic has participated renowned institutions such as Bank of America as it presented a report on the virtues of this type of investment in the long term.

The historical highs that have been reached by these assets, work as a proof of betting on this path, they are more interesting financial markets than the traditional ones, so they can be exploited as part of a digital opportunity that can change lives.

The analysis presented on cryptocurrencies, works to settle this concept, but at the same time it is required to have the strength to wait for the falls that are presented, where a golden rule to follow is to wait for the price to decrease to be able to be part of the purchase of cryptocurrencies, that way you do not let yourself be clouded by this option.

Business reviews and studies point out that there is still a huge fear about investing in cryptocurrencies, especially about losing your investment completely, as it is also a market with constant deep recessions, which is why it is called a volatile environment.

But dips over the cryptocurrency world can turn into a quality jump, it is an avenue to profit and is described as a timely buy, it is profitable as long as you can dodge desperate selling, by putting that aside you can stumble upon the best days over this medium.

Investing in difficult times is a help to succumb over losses, bear markets is a timely start to carry out a long term investment, that is one way to form a complete strategy on this medium, but it has been proven that it takes at least 1,100 days to recover from losses.

All this depends on the behavior of cryptocurrencies, which is what demonstrates the pace at which the asset moves, where volatility is a quality to live with, especially because of that dreaded bearish balance, this pushes towards the materialization of rapid recoveries as well, beyond what is thought.

Forming a long-term cryptocurrency investment strategy

The market behind cryptocurrencies has a very high mobility, this is due to its growth, but without fixed trends, therefore hodl is one of the tasks to master, although it can be complicated for beginners, it is a situation where the first thing is to assume the type of losses you face.

But there is no certainty in the market, it is a feeling that must be dealt with, because it is impossible to know for sure the type of direction that an investment or the market itself will generate, even if some gurus offer signals or predictions, these estimates may not work out in the end.

Therefore, the best answer is to analyze and form your own strategy that allows you to earn money in the long term, this is what opens the opportunities for profits to materialize by a safer way or at least by the hand of your own decisions, for this you must estimate some aspects.

As you know and study certain points, you can generate profits to form a healthy and well nourished portfolio, where you must eliminate certain negative aspects such as the problems of human psychology, no idea is infallible, but it can be a strategy formed by golden rules when investing.

Delineating some best practices can help you avoid a total loss, even finding profitable opportunities that are eye-catching, but there is no need to focus entirely on everything that can go wrong, but also no need to be under the illusion of buying and keeping your money intact.

The most recommended or the most assumed position is to do hodling, where the recommendations exposed in Coinmarketcap are followed as a way to form the cryptocurrency portfolio, following the top exposed in recognized platforms, but starting from the quality that there are many young assets and can result in everything.

Thinking about a strategy plan is essential and will give you a lot of benefits, you can follow these comparison lines or concepts to have a firm step to follow:

- **Building a long-term investment strategy**

The main thing to consider is that the capital you are going to invest should not be indispensable for your living expenses, that is to say, it is money that you are willing to lose, because they are funds that you will not be able to resort to until the estimated period of time or a desired profit in terms of percentage has elapsed.

The intention is that you do not think about the fund that is not available, in the same way it is vital to know in depth the project on which you are going to invest, because on this depends the growth or progress of such asset, to reach that point of conviction you must ask yourself the type of problems it solves and the industry to which it is dedicated.

Knowledge is also important when exploring who is behind the project, that way when these answers are presented you can avoid losing money, especially due to lack of knowledge, this part of your strategy should incorporate the big movements that are presented in the market.

The broad future of cryptocurrencies depends on the basis that exists on a project, this starting point is fundamental so that in the long term the promising side can be visualized, in the same way it works for medium-term investments, since blockchain technology depends on these evolution factors.

The influence of these issues is established to stay over time, i.e. cryptocurrencies are part of everyday life, so betting on this way is an improvement for anyone who gets the right investment, having this in mind opens the way to invest systematically to buy when the price is at the lowest point.

Then selling concentrates on the overvalued moments, but getting it right in a precise way is what takes a lot of work or vision, which for some may be like impossible but investment entails methodology to get results, the essential thing is that you do not worry about some movements made in the market.

Always the cryptocurrency environment is going to be classified as a volatile environment, so you are always going to be exposed to constant stressful situations, but when you accept it and figure out how to avoid it, you can deal with whatever happens, to the point of ignoring whatever happens, that's the kind of wellness an investor can consider.

In long term investments, you must live with a concept called "Market Timing", it is an illusory ability to find the direction in which the market is going to move, but it is described as illusory since it is a practically impossible action, no matter how many years you own about this alternative.

When you try to win this type of domain, you can fall into a series of disastrous steps, which can lead you to lose money, so from the beginning you must understand that this effort may be in vain because it is complex, in the end it is an intuition itself.

• The tool of self-knowledge

In the cryptocurrency market you must confront an important fact, it has nothing to do entirely with volatility, much less with scammers, but directly with your own emotions and the beliefs you have about this medium, for this reason the strategies have or retain the intention to control the feelings.

During the decision making process, the most correct thing to do is to remain in a neutral state, since you will be part of a market that does not have a rational behavior, but in a short period of time some news comes out, and for that reason you should not run out to sell, much less without thinking about what it means for you.

In the long term you should operate with a higher level of rationality, as this quality can then be used to avoid being intimidated by any movement, because fear can lead to the following common mistakes:

1. You invest in an asset that you don't know, or don't understand.
2. You don't think about diversifying your investment.
3. You buy and sell continuously.
4. You employ leverage and make short purchases.

It is also true that the human side, in some occasions can be uncontrollable, since normally more value is given to the emotional side of each step or decision, in this case it would be in hooking too much to some currency, or in a type of movement in the market.

That kind of view should apply when a person declares that a currency should go up, just because they like the concept or something similar, because when the opposite happens, you're just going to want to extend some excuse to say it was an unusual move, but you never assume you were wrong for holding that position.

The market has a behavior like any other, beyond the type of feelings that you can develop for it, for this reason the rational side cannot disappear for any reason.

- **Research on the projects to be invested**

Once you invest for the long term, there is no need to stick to candlesticks, much less to the trends that are marked on a chart, but on the key points that exist about the cryptocurrency project, so a personal research helps you to get answers, it is not a complicated step and it is very useful.

Within the research you carry out you must comply with some characteristics, these must be studied in depth and analyzed to take a position on any cryptocurrency, within which the following points stand out:

1. What and who is behind the project.
2. The asset and its value is sufficiently clear.
3. How the project works, discover all the technical aspects.
4. The type of problem it solves and its association with real problems.
5. Determine if it is a real problem.
6. The industry in which the asset is engaged.
7. The partnerships behind a cryptocurrency.

This path makes it easier for you to recognize the technology that exists on cryptoassets, since the industry that supports these values or imposes a purpose on the coins possesses a determining weight, but at the moment of waiting for profits you should stay away from these points, likewise from articles that suggest any investment.

Reading some social network is not enough, they are purely opinions, so a research on your own can open the way, since the responsibility to invest is on your side, regardless of what they can recommend.

- **The diversified investment portfolio**

A powerful weapon in the cryptocurrency environment is diversification, as it is the best way for risks to go down, because no matter how much time you have read about a project, there is still a lot to learn, especially because overcoming the uncertainty phase depends on facing risks you don't know about.

By buying different assets there is a possibility of decreasing the margin of error, but the future cannot be assured no matter how promising a cryptocurrency turns out to be, as it can be worth a few cents at the beginning and then increase greatly or be a flop, anything can happen.

Currently as different currencies are found, you can think about betting on the best ones, but there are threats to keep in mind that are capable of collapsing any forecast, since no type of industry is completely improved and guaranteed by a cryptocurrency, because the other industries are a competition itself.

In the case of IOTA at the beginning it did not use blockchain technology, but currently there are Circle and Hashgraph, the same happens with Ripple that was dedicated to support the banking system, but through Stellar it seeks to obtain a share of the market of the former.

The search for a balanced portfolio, is through two alternatives, firstly, by keeping a similar amount of money on each of the cryptocurrencies that are part of your portfolio, or secondly you can have several kinds of cryptocurrencies, these two approaches are recommended.

A basic step is to create the investment portfolio through different types of cryptocurrencies, then you can focus on holding a distributed investment in equal or balanced shares, for this you can take as a reference a fund of $10,000 USD and allocate it to 10 cryptocurrencies with a value of around $1,000 USD on each one.

The types of cryptocurrencies are as follows:

1. Tokens that are asset-based.

The asset-based token is booming and issues a representation on the value of another asset class, this applies on gold, art pieces, fiat currency, among others, this modality allows investing in assets that are not cryptocurrencies themselves, but through the same you can bet on them.

They are known as Stable Coins or stable coins, it is a way to acquire these goods in a simple way, so that instead of buying a work of art worth millions, you can have a part of it through the tokens, it is a fraction of prices that makes everything more interesting and within your reach.

The same happens when you want to invest in gold, because you don't get a physical asset or worry about storage, it is a much simpler way for you to be part of the most attractive assets in the world.

2. Tokens related to values.

Value tokens are developed with the function of obtaining funds, that means that they do not provide any access to a service, but allow participation in the growth of the project, and it is also a benefit because if the token is removed over time you will get compensation.

This type of cryptocurrency is not as popular as the others, but the attention must be directed to the regulations that these assets have, so it can be a greater risk than other options, because the level of uncertainty is complex to reduce.

The security issue does not limit that this is an interesting type of investment, because in the midst of fundraising it is a solution with great potential, helping to form a better structure of shareholders within the company, you can review the issue of the legal framework to take these steps with confidence.

3. Utility tokens.

The tokens corresponding to utilities are built or dedicated for dapps, i.e. to have full access to the services provided by the platforms, their design is purely focused on a Blockchain application, it is considered a type of tokens that are risky, due to the stage they are in.

In the case of use on Ethereum still presents scalability problems, and another negative aspect is not knowing the platform chosen in the long term as the favorite, since it may be an accentuated preference on NEO and then on Ethereum, there is no guarantee of this, so the development of each application is doomed to these doubts.

It all depends on the work behind a platform, since, if in the case of Ethereum the scalability detail is solved, it means that the service provided over the apps will not be the most appropriate or sought after, therefore when an efficient service is delivered what is going to happen is that the token is going to grow and provide rewards.

4. Coins of certain platforms.

These currencies are completely associated with Blockchain technology and have among their functions the creation of applications on it, these are known as Ethereum, Cardano, Lisk, NEO, and others, as the platform is used much more, there will be more demand for cryptocurrencies.

Because cryptocurrencies are used in applications, which means that they can be purchased in an ICO, this type of currency has been considered as one of the most secure currencies and has a great potential for further growth, because its blockchain promotes decentralized solutions.

It is complicated to determine which cryptocurrency has the best development, but with a thorough research you can diversify your options, it is a category to discover in depth, especially to use in your favor the advantage that they do not have regulations and maintain their full form because they are created to acquire services.

5. Transactional currencies.

They are a kind of cryptocurrencies that fulfill the function of providing value, a clear example of this concept is Bitcoin as it is an asset that meets these conditions, the same happens in the case of Litecoin, Zcash, Dash and others, many of these have a high level of popularity, where many value the type of privacy.

Above these mentioned options you can find other categories, but they are only formal classifications and when it comes to investing you can take into account the above types of cryptocurrencies, in the case of ICOs they fit with any of the mentioned classifications, it is an offering that varies.

Knowing the concept of each type of cryptocurrency, you can diversify by betting on each type of asset in percentages according to your level of confidence or how promising that concept is for you, it can be 30% to transactional coins, 25% to platform coins, 10% to value and utility tokens and 25% to asset-backed ones.

The favorite options to complete with that percentage, are estimated in Stellar, Ethereum, Bitcoin, Cardano, Monero, NEO, IOTA, and EOS, this is an example that you can adjust to your preference, you must think of a balance that can adjust to you, besides assuming the risk of each cryptocurrency according to its concept or project.

The most common alternative is to have a balanced proportion of funds, but for no reason you can do it in an excessive way, and choose to sell those that have risen too much, to start buying others that are low over the market, so that the portfolio remains alive acquiring a percentage of profit.

- **Other strategy components**

Upon completion of a research on the world of assets you can confidently choose the cryptocurrency, to proceed to other elements of the strategy to invest in the long term, this allows to fulfill the purpose of maintaining discipline in every step or decision as it is the important aspect so that losses are not generated.

When you don't pay attention to discipline, you won't have the ability to suppress your emotions about your investment or financial decisions, this is what allows you to get a chance to reap profits when a bull market presents itself, but if you sell early or inappropriately you will regret it.

The best tips or actions to complement a long-term cryptocurrency investment are as follows:

1. Choose a period to study the portfolio in depth until it generates enough security, the same goes for measuring progress and making decisions about it, this can be done once a week or once a month, the important thing is that it is a comfortable day so that there is no rush and you make a good analysis.
2. Use an application to carry out a deep price analysis, a good alternative is Altpocket, as it allows you to visualize the performance of the entire portfolio options, it is a broad view that includes a variety of cryptocurrencies.
3. Create an average price range, this works to measure the maximum amount of investment you have available for this purpose, as well as the time over which you are going to keep that investment.

4. Decide on the strategy to obtain profits, i.e. determine the moment when you are going to sell the cryptocurrency to reap profits, and how much you are going to sell, the most advisable is that the portfolio should be formed by percentage on which you must have perseverance to sell in a balanced way.

This type of data is estimated to have clarity on the steps to follow, so that no scenario takes you by surprise, by means of a support you will act at the right time.

- **Estimates to purchase**

Having these basic rules makes it easier to have everything clear when buying cryptocurrencies to build your portfolio or portfolio, it is best that purchases are made gradually, so you can reduce volatility, because identifying the best time is an impossible task.

But it is best to buy a little at a time, as this does not negatively affect your funds or investment, you can reduce risks in this way, plus the average price makes it easier for you to buy different cryptocurrency options, instead of placing all your investment at once.

Following this kind of steps allows you to reach a good price, and at the same time you can decrease the emotions about these operations, without thinking about the future situation of the market, you just need to set different periods to buy without paying attention to the kind of current situation that is on the market.

The program or average price, can be measured by the frequency on which you plan to invest, it can be weekly, monthly and yearly, this goes in combination with the amount to invest on each of the rounds of purchases, betting on an average cost is an important way to reduce the risk in any situation.

When you are investing for the long term, what you are aiming for is that the value of the cryptocurrency can increase, that kind of view decreases over your mete any pressure, another option is to buy all at once when you see a remarkably low price, but this step carries a lot of risks.

But when you buy all at once and the price declines, you may think about selling at once, as this is a much more complex psychological position for you, while buying through different prices does not affect or generate that internal struggle to detect the right time.

At the moment of setting the orders should not be carried out under the market price, since at the beginning it may be a convenient action, but this decreases the profit due to the percentage issue, also when you opt for some exchanges such as Kucoin, Binance, Bittrex and Poloniex, you can find prices that are not the best in the market.

- **Rebalancing the portfolio**

Rebalancing the portfolio is an activity that is conceived as an asset management process, this entails selling certain cryptocurrencies that have increased a lot in value, thereby buying others to balance, that way the assets that are within the investment portfolio do not lose importance.

When a cryptocurrency is reduced to 400%, and others have stability, it means that the asset can become 40% of your portfolio, even if at the beginning you only had 10% for this type of asset, one way to see these changes is by means of a pie chart.

This method is a sample of monitoring so that you get all the information of the assets you have, a first action is to sell the portion of cryptocurrencies that have grown at high levels in recent times, this kind of step should be carried out on a weekly, monthly or semi-annual basis.

But the most advisable thing is not to choose short periods, since due to the commissions it is not profitable, at least once every three months is the most optimal, without falling into any volatile situation to make any decision, because that only leaves bad results during the purchase and sale.

- **Acquiring the proceeds**

Taking profits may seem simple at first glance, especially when you realize that your investment has grown, since the objective is to obtain a point of profitability, but this is a complicated path and in the long run it must be sustained, unless some conditions have changed drastically.

If you do not need that fund that is invested, it is better to observe a normal development to wait for the growth of each cryptocurrency, because it is useless to withdraw the money as soon as there is a single rise, and miss the highs that arise, it is difficult to control the desire to sell when you notice that it is beginning to increase.

It may be greedy to aim for a percentage of profit, but if you really believe it based on a project you can take this step, although you must take into account that it is not an easy point to determine, and selling in a hurry does not make much sense, although you may need the fund, it is best to wait and receive the reward of the results.

This type of strategy is what allows you to leave aside the moments of fear, as these are situations that can limit the progress of profits, so you should not get carried away by news or by the evolution of the price, because these ideas only lead you to make a mistake.

It is essential to reiterate that a good research can work as a key point to invest in the long term, but accepting that not all the time you are going to be right, but a deep study about the projects helps you to achieve profits, instead of obsessing with reviewing the charts because it depends on the investment modality.

Examples and visions for long-term investment in cryptocurrencies

A long term investment in cryptocurrencies is estimated as a long period of time, it can be composed between 12 months and over 18 months, but the most advisable in the world of cryptocurrencies is to support an even longer period of time, the usual is to establish a strategy that allows you to reap profits that generate peace of mind.

As you can take advantage of time, you can let it be an element that works as an ally for you, in that way you can materialize the profitability of your actions, but this is built through a strong investment, that level of constancy should not receive or count on large oscillations.

The search for profits is based on the use of cash flows, these are offered or disposed of by the assets that you place in your portfolio, thus obtaining a revaluation on market assets, the big difference with short-term investments is that these are much more volatile.

On the other hand, in the long term, the first step is to recognize the value of diversification, but this requires a detailed study of both risk and return, in order to understand what is at stake so that the money can be allocated with greater confidence.

The approach to a long-term investment should follow a much more measured profile, because this is the best way for you to make more stable steps, to the point of being an investment that will sustain many years without serious losses, the assets need to be solvent in order to yield returns.

- **Long-term investments that are profitable**

One aspect to constantly deal with is risk, as well as that human response of minimizing it to open yourself to the long-term mode, but it is also important to take care of profitability because it goes hand in hand with the risk taken, so most people prefer to focus on low-risk options.

But the duty requires to be placed on an asset that is recognizable as profitable, for this you can adjust the risk along with the portfolio or assets you have in sight, in addition there is the option to combine it with assets that are safe to balance the final result while keeping the risk in an optimal point.

Therefore, portfolios need to be diversified, but not in individual assets, but look for equities, as this is a way where you get a higher return, and in the long term this view is ideal because the assets perform better compared to other financial instruments.

The combination of assets allows you to achieve stability, and at the same time consistency, this is known as a winning financial formula, this way is ideal to constitute a strong investment option to complete a competent portfolio, by means of these options:

1. **Dividend investment**

It is exposed as a dedicated strategy for long-term investments, at the same time it is a simple and effective modality at the same time, it is a dynamic through which the hypothesis of betting on the profits of some companies is pursued, especially those that are available for the shareholder structure.

It is known as a strategy based on equity investments, so it is special for cryptocurrencies that are anchored to a similar project, since the yield of such shares can be transformed into variable income because the dividends that can be collected are not established on some contract.

It all depends on the type of profits that the company itself has obtained from any business, so you should prefer a company that increases the level of profits, this is directly noticeable on the dividends, it works as a way of increasing income over time.

The market oscillations in this case are not so important, they only influence when a stock loses its value, but this only means that it is time to buy, as this leads to a highly profitable investment vehicle, every investor can take advantage of depreciations to enjoy higher profitability.

2. **Replicate an index**

In the subject of investment it is crucial to investigate some funds, because it is possible to replicate the behavior of a market index, this can be developed in a fixed or variable income way, therefore when obtaining or participating in that fund and creating a portfolio of assets, it can be composed by means of elements denominated as indexed funds.

This financial path is very useful, because it is about replicating the economy without the need to worry so much about the formation of the portfolio, it is a management known as a passive philosophy, the index is a measure that is defined as a weighting or an average, therefore the degree of volatility is lower.

The oscillations that are generated on these assets, with the ability to compensate each other, so that the risk is completely diminished is a formula to fight the market, which involves accepting a lot of risk, but knowing the market impulses can frame a horizon.

3. **Alternative investment funds**

When you cannot find a fund to replicate the exact behavior, you can think of an investment through income funds which is variable, it is a way to reinvest in returns on the fund itself, using what has been produced, therefore it becomes a very useful financial instrument through long-term investment.

4. Value Investing

It is a strategy with great popularity thanks to the sponsorship of Warren Buffett, which has been responsible for creating a financial institution in the world as a religion itself, it is an alternative where the choice of a variable income fund is established, for this a valuation of the project behind the asset is developed.

As you can practice some appraisal you can recognize the value behind the target of a stock, that way you can compare the result obtained with the price that can quote that asset, in addition you can get some kind of discount which is known as a fundamental aspect.

Most effective strategies when investing in Cardano

Cardano is extremely interesting, it has its birth in this financial environment since 2017 and since that moment it has kept climbing important positions, this goes hand in hand with the concept that cryptocurrencies have since they have a price fluctuation and can be unattainable for some.

But beyond some of the characteristics of this market, there is a wide boldness on the part of users to bet on digital assets, and this has produced an important gain on weighty options such as Cardano, through its cryptocurrency ADA.

Regardless of the fact that the world of cryptocurrencies is unregulated, the important thing is to determine the trends that appear on this medium, where ADA is positioned as an attractive bet, every investor should consider this type of opportunity which is represented as a blockchain designed by Input Output Hong Kong (IOHK).

The interest of investors is becoming a reality on this project, the scale of Cardano in the world is of great notoriety, since it has reached striking positions in the rankings, many express that this is due to the fact that its arrival has coincided with other launches on this medium, Ada as a cryptocurrency has skyrocketed its value.

The token classification reaffirms this alternative as one of the best 10 on the market capitalization, therefore all the concentration is dedicated to the Cardano blockchain, which has a two-layer structure, one called Cardano Setlemet Layer, which is in charge of carrying out cryptoasset transactions.

The other layer that is part of the block is called as Cardano Computation Layer, this part is dedicated to implement the applications and the participation of developers, so it is a novelty that is appreciated by all investors, because other cryptocurrencies such as Bitcoin, Ripple and others are the ones that use blockchain.

Cardano has progressively become a very exciting asset, and large exchanges have facilitated it to be an affordable purchase for every user, this is an important gap to invest in the long term, even if it does not have a long history, since it has not been created for more than 5 years.

You can bet on some advanced tool to measure the risk of this investment, this works as a protection for you to reach important positions at a volatile level, obtaining the movements that this asset has developed in the market, by observing these results you can measure the risks and take responsibility for it.

Different communities share the criterion of studying this cryptocurrency in depth, you can build a great strategy to invest for all the high, this is known as Popular Investors and users CopyFunds as a kind of advice to form an investment portfolio.

What to keep in mind when investing in cryptocurrencies for the long term

The return that exists on the cryptocurrency market is striking, as it is able to provide up to 900%, that level of return is not evident in any other financial environment, because with a good guess you can invest $500 USD and then get as a result up to $5,000 USD, that is why it is implemented more regularly.

A long term investment is an optimal measure, but it requires care because it moves very fast, therefore the inclusion of strategies is a requirement, while still being beneficial to increase your wealth, as these markets present an upward trend as time goes by, this is part of the motivation.

In addition, investing in this type of assets does not involve so many commissions, because exchanges generate a minimum amount compared to other traditional investment methods, and it is a less risky measure because it depends on your pulse, i.e. under your own actions is the level of profit or loss to be faced.

But it is important that you possess a stake within the cryptocurrency world with a portfolio, along with other elements that are able to provide a much more in-depth reading that measure the potential behind such assets, this is a starting point for you to research more about it and you can create a course of action.

- **Long-term value indicators**

In order for you to keep track of the value of an asset over the long term, you can develop the following supports or measurement tools that provide you with a more accurate view of what is happening within this market:

1. **Market Share**

It is described as a market share that allows defining the proportion level for the market capitalization to develop, this cryptocurrency information is fundamental to carry out an exhaustive monitoring, since when there is a notorious market share it is usually a dominance.

The level of market capitalization refers to the space to know the level of viability that exists in the long term, so that you can create a portfolio that has a future and above all the possibility of growth.

2. **Utility value**

When you want to know if a cryptocurrency is going to hold up, from the time you buy it until a few years down the road, you can question and research the usefulness of the asset, as well as check if it is an active market with users, as these are key points to know if it is likely to be an adopted asset.

An example of real utility is Ethereum, because it allows you to create decentralized applications, meaning that there is a great convenience or need behind it, that way it is easy to aspire to keep it as it responds to that utility, and so you can include an asset on your portfolio.

3. **Transaction volume**

It is an indicator used to know if a cryptocurrency is really being used, this can be determined under the transaction volume, especially within its historical level is also a reflection of the importance it has on the market, it is also a sign that this will increase and reaffirms how scalable it is to hold that investment.

4. **Technology development**

It is considered as a key aspect to measure about cryptocurrencies, since it has an analysis on the technology that supports such asset, this is a signal to recognize if it is an alternative with probability of success based on its technological development, it is also a way on which transactions are developed, the more efficient, the more the numbers increase.

5. **Market news**

In case a cryptocurrency is under difficulties, you can study the whole issue and determine the level of the problem involved, as long as it is not an impediment that limits the long-term viability, you can continue to be guided by other details, because the media role cannot be above the previous study.

The important thing is that you know what is happening to issue any reaction or inquire about news of future releases, this completely affects the price of the asset, for this reason it is a wake that should not be overlooked, being up to date is a great reference to form and make decisions to the asset portfolio.

These are some basic indicators, they are a sign of viability before lifting a finger, at the beginning you can keep this in mind to have a solid portfolio, as long as you can sustain a percentage of such assets according to the results generated through research.

- **Passion for risk**

There is no doubt that the determination of the long-term investment span is measured according to the exposure of the chosen cryptocurrency, but it also goes hand in hand with the risk capacity you tolerate, i.e. the more risk you take, the more you can get a winning movement, especially if compared to what a traditional market leaves.

- **The most popular projections**

Online you can find a lot of recommendations to create your portfolio, with differences and personal preferences that bring out the best options that exist to reap a good profit margin, those online schemes are popular, but you can use them as inspiration.

1. **Bitcoin**

First of all, in every investment portfolio the Bitcoin is persistently placed, it is a base asset over other cryptocurrencies with the same decentralized classification, since 2009 as a pioneer it works as an inspiration itself in the financial world, due to its wide trajectory it is used in more and more trades.

The cryptocurrency market is volatile, as part of its main specifications, so you can establish a low-risk portfolio or one that fits your business vision, but in the case of Bitcoin in the long term it can be a very balanced asset, it is clearly noticeable on the attention it receives from the news.

2. Bitcoin Cash

A second option is Bitcoin Cash, this is an alternative similar to the concept of Bitcoin, the difference is that it has a block size of 8MB, while bitcoin is located in 1MB, this means that it has a higher speed to process transactions and at a low cost.

By keeping in mind these distinctive movements between Bitcoin and Bitcoin Cash, it becomes clear that they are not related, but one clear movement is that when Bitcoin is rising it means that the price of Bitcoin Cash is moving down, this type of data can be used as a strategy to offset an adverse Bitcoin movement.

3. Ethereum

Ethereum is a very different option to Bitcoin, since its function is to allow the development of dApps using smart contracts, the currency of this project is called Ether, it is a promising environment for everything it provides in terms of proposition or initiative.

4. **Litecoin**

It is recognized as a promotion similar to Bitcoin's gold status, on the other hand, it represents a hard fork coming from Bitcoin, there is no doubt that Litecoin can be used as a value exchange currency, but the block generation time is at least 2.5 minutes, if compared to Bitcoin possess a difference of 10 minutes.

The design of this asset is based on a hash algorithm (Scrypt), which is used to produce or generate the blockchain, which is why it is classified as one of the most modern cryptocurrencies.

5. **Monero**

Monero has a great similarity to Bitcoin, because its function is to be an exchange of value, but its difference is that it has become an asset that seeks at all costs to ensure the privacy of users participating in the blockchain, through an address mechanism that cannot be detected.

Anonymity is increasingly sought after and this becomes a reality through this way, so your address is not exposed for any reason, instead if you invest in Bitcoin it can be tracked, this is essential in an environment where there are more and more regulations and privacy is useful when engaging in transactions.

6. Zcash

Zcash complies with the same parameters of Monero, since it seeks to take care of privacy to its maximum expression, the anonymity of users is a highly demanded requirement, it is a medium that facilitates the exchange of information without revealing the identities of the participants.

Generally speaking, investing in the cryptocurrency market is emotional, but you must keep in mind that you require security over the assets, which means that the choice of the wallet is a fundamental step, so you are going to participate in an investment that will test your emotions.

This asset class provides a higher level of return, for this reason it is inspiring, the abandonment over traditional means of investment is due to the advantages that this opportunity provides and the technological support, this becomes a reality once you get a high level strategy to overcome and resist the market.

Considerations and doubts about long-term trading

For a long time the idea of investing in the short term has been popular, because it is a way to reap a striking level of profit in a short time, but in the long term you can find lower risks and control over the level of profit to which you are aiming, these are qualities to keep in mind between one or the other measure.

Obtaining money through Bitcoin trading, as well as through other cryptocurrencies, is not such a distant or simple goal. First of all, it depends on two aspects: the time you dedicate to achieve it, and the risk you are able to assume in the process.

The term always goes hand in hand with the type of risk to be assumed, but to make a more informed decision on one option or another you can consider the following points:

- **Watch out for fraudulent options**

The wide world of Bitcoin is made up of important alternatives, sometimes they have more to do with investing than selling, on the other hand, you should be careful with the amount of trading geniuses or gurus that you will find in this medium, because they offer you to invest in some cryptocurrencies as a help, but they are the opposite.

The situations you have to deal with are varied, because they can be scams, and on the other hand it can also be the creation of a positive trend by intensifying prices, i.e. they are plans where the clients themselves in addition to paying, act as an intermediary trading for them to obtain profits on their portfolio.

The attraction should be placed directly on the information content, because it is an academic training that is provided with the purpose of achieving a better return, especially when it is a long-term investment, this is the best way to learn, beyond the fact that it is tempting to pay for data or signals.

- **The present vs. tomorrow**

The data around these trends in the cryptocurrency market, and in the world of traditional finance, is a means where it is evident that you must implement novel strategies, because if you stick to past practices, you are only going to get bad results, and a general rule is to diversify your investment.

Through different cryptocurrencies it is possible to take advantage of a higher level of compound interest, this can be realized through certain platforms of the level or importance of Binance, thus returns begin to materialize without having to take security risks.

At the level of investors, it is exposed that trading is very risky for you at the level of health, because the usual thing is that you only get a lower return than what is exposed or found in the market, so the idea of investing on a cryptocurrency ecosystem subjects you to many steps and measures to overcome the fear.

Learning the skill of investing in cryptocurrencies is a progressive step, i.e. it is about escalation and above all discovery, so on average you may run into decisions that are not profitable, but it is in persistence over losses that you can reap gains, leaving aside the stumbles of the past.

It can be seen that, for common investors, these steps are not profitable, especially when you add up all the aspects involved and the commissions, this is raised in the transactions you make, where the margin of loss is high, although in the long run you get rid of this kind of headache.

- **Preference over the long road in investments**

The data behind long-term investment in cryptocurrencies imposes that short-term risks can be completely eliminated, multiplying the capital you own, so the key can be on the speed of trading, in addition to the establishment of safe options for the return on investment to be present.

The long-term return generates higher percentages in some cases, also some exchanges have the option to provide compound interest, because in the case of Binance generates 5% on many of the cryptocurrencies offered, so the simple fact of keeping cryptocurrencies can provide annual returns.

Predictions favor long-term investments much more, because if you opt for a short term, the risk increases because, if you harvest a positive percentage of profit, you can then lose it in another investment, while in the long term you have the control to get out when it has increased to the level or margin you expect.

The investment role of social trading

In cryptocurrency investment it is vital to recognize what you should do and the consequences, that way you can clarify the "how" to invest by following the right steps, to make this a reality experts issue certain tips, so that the investment community can choose the right cryptocurrency.

The importance of cryptocurrencies today transcends to be a very popular financial instrument, especially because it is a way to break the chains of centralization, you just have to overcome the fear of volatility as a first step to start betting on assets and grow as Bitcoin and Ether.

The records of cryptocurrencies clearly expose the opportunity to invest in a project, you can also follow by some stable options that are useful for conservatives, where it highlights the role of DAI or the Tether itself that is anchored to the dollar and its value.

This type of trend at international level is a live bet, above some uncertainty, this can be discussed through the study of mercadocripto, where statistics become a very reason to trust this type of financial opportunity, generating a higher level of confidence on users towards currencies.

But the real reason why more people decide to invest in this medium, is under the conformation of long term strategies, this is mostly due to the distrust that exists about the traditional financial system, but the best way to leave aside this barrier the first step is to buy them.

On the other hand, you must think about how to use the asset, by means of holder defined as a holder or holder of the asset, and then become a trader or operator, this magic formula becomes a reality through social trading, this is about having the ability to use different tools.

The way to reduce the risk is by means of different measurement elements, which at the same time increases the learning curve, so you must know or have these measures in mind:

- **The role of social trading**

It is basically to duplicate the digital portfolio owned by a reference person, it must be someone who is recognized in the financial world, in addition to having proven results in real facts, so that you follow their investments betting on the assets that they consider as assets.

Getting a profitable alternative is possible through this way, but assuming the responsibility of your choice, since this does not have an absolute guarantee, you can win and lose equally, in the cryptocurrency environment no decision is safe, but at least you are following an expert's strategy.

The mood can be much calmer knowing that you are relying on reliable data, rather than exposing yourself to too much market risk, and this idea helps you to be bold.

- **How to be part of social trading**

In the midst of a lot of trading platforms, you will get a section for social activities, this is what allows the development of social trading, it is a way for you not to have to take steps alone in this medium, as investing can be a challenge for you completely.

Social trading is becoming more and more widely used, according to data from PrimeXBT and iProUP, which reports that more than 9,000 users are dedicated to copying strategies using a capital of around 10 million dollars, obtaining important profitability results of up to 5,560% depending on the choice.

But to achieve positive results it is feasible to opt for portfolios that are high risk, which from the beginning indicates that there are many loss factors involved, but a portfolio that is conservative can provide a return of at least 30% of a monthly income.

The profit of this method is 100% real, but it does not exempt you from losing a considerable amount of money depending on your choices, in all kinds of investments you must contemplate the risks to reap profits, there is no sure way to get money, without exposure you will not be able to achieve success.

The steps to use this strategy when investing under social trading are simple and can be summarized in these measures:

1. Through PrimeXBT for example, you can enter and have access to the tab called Covesting, on this option you will find a large number of options to form strategies ordered according to the type of qualities you choose.
2. In the middle of the selection, you can choose to filter the degree of risk to which you are facing, this goes hand in hand with the time through which you are going to operate, and without forgetting to confirm the experience or

importance of the administrator of the strategy on the platform.
3. Find a suitable option for your profile, you can get some quick profit through strategies that are high risk, as well as long term, that way funds are spread more safely.

The type of social platform is what provides a character about the investment, i.e. it translates into a way to check the level of confidence that the forecast has, since, if it is an environment with little reputation, it is not a good option to spread your assets, you must also maintain a fluid communication with investors.

In the midst of the community, you can sustain yourself in the face of setbacks in the market, but it can also be counterproductive because it can awaken your fears, so you can read and take care of the anonymity side, so that you are more focused on operations only.

But a key to this option is not to stick to a single strategy, much less to a single character, also some earnings can be used as a lure so you should not get carried away by promises or much less, the concentration should be on the results, prefer only managers with more seniority.

The "HODL or die" trend

Long term cryptocurrency investment recommendation is a daily advice on any social media, they are outstanding financial movements because some historical margin can leave you a considerable profit, but you should also expect some drops, this means losses, not an opportunity to buy because you can expect something to close you from other assets.

One enemy to confront is the fear or impulse to make sales in a recession of great magnitude, especially when it is historically recognized that after these scenarios there is a positive jump, so that a hasty sale does not leave any kind of profit, but rather losses of a higher level.

Staying invested income over difficult times is a fundamental rule for long term participation in cryptocurrencies, you need to stay calm and wait for a longer time span than 1000 days to recover, but this can vary over the performance margins as very drastic changes are seen.

Hodling is a preferred practice in all senses, it is an ecosystem in which you are going to encounter growth percentages that you did not imagine from the beginning, therefore time is the best advisor for you to obtain profits, without losing sight of patience as a lifesaver to wait for the moment to sell.

Measures to invest in Bitcoin for the long term

There is no doubt that a cryptocurrency of great relevance as Bitcoin has certain details not to overlook, so you can not forget the training on cryptocurrencies through courses where special strategies are organized for the assets that you have in mind to include in your portfolio.

A means of analysis is installed on the Bitcoin network, since this control is what allows to visualize the movement that this popular asset can have throughout the world, in addition the users themselves are the ones who maintain control of the transactions by validation on the blockchain.

The operation of Bitcoin depends on the number of points that allow or accept this means of payment, on this side arises a kind of security to bet on this asset, it is conceived as a reliable means is part of the blockchain technology, it is a book where each of the digital movements are housed.

Another measure to be part of the investment on Bitcoin is under mining, since after all they are assets that have encrypted code, and the time involved depends directly on the mining power, but the profitability depends on the devices you use.

The first steps is to buy Bitcoin and choose the safest wallet, then the operation goes hand in hand with the actions of the stock management, for this you must follow the evolution of that asset, until it reaches an opportune moment to sell and that makes a difference on the day you bought it.

www.ingramcontent.com/pod-product-compliance
Lightning Source LLC
Chambersburg PA
CBHW070454220526
45466CB00004B/1818